DARWIN AND EVOLUTION

BULLET GUIDE

James Napier

Hodder Education, 338 Euston Road, London NW1 3BH

Hodder Education is an Hachette UK company

First published in UK 2011 by Hodder Education

This edition published 2011

Copyright © 2011 James Napier

The moral rights of the author have been asserted

Database right Hodder Education (makers)

Artworks (internal and cover): Peter Lubach

Cover concept design: Two Associates

British Library Cataloguing in Publication Data: a catalogue record for this title is available from the British Library.

10 9 8 7 6 5 4 3 2 1

The publisher has used its best endeavours to ensure that any website addresses referred to in this book are correct and active at the time of going to press. However, the publisher and the author have no responsibility for the websites and can make no guarantee that a site will remain live or that the content will remain relevant, decent or appropriate.

The publisher has made every effort to mark as such all words which it believes to be trademarks. The publisher should also like to make it clear that the presence of a word in the book, whether marked or unmarked, in no way affects its legal status as a trademark.

Every reasonable effort has been made by the publisher to trace the copyright holders of material in this book. Any errors or omissions should be notified in writing to the publisher, who will endeavour to rectify the situation for any reprints and future editions.

Hachette UK's policy is to use papers that are natural, renewable and recyclable products and made from wood grown in sustainable forests. The logging and manufacturing processes are expected to conform to the environmental regulations of the country of origin.

www.hoddereducation.co.uk

Typeset by Stephen Rowling/Springworks

Printed in Spain

Contents

Acknowledgements

I am grateful to Harry Scoble from Hodder Education for giving me the opportunity to write this brief overview of such an important contemporary topic. Thanks to Sam Richardson and his colleagues, and also to Máire, Catherine and Aisling for their immense support. Particular thanks to Brian Rushton, who ignited the spark of biological curiosity in me that made the writing of this book both a possibility and a pleasure.

About the author

Dr James Napier completed his D. Phil. on 'Variation and Adaptation in *Allium ursinum*' (wild garlic) at the University of Ulster in 1994. Much of this research focused on the ecological and evolutionary adaptations that enable this species to dominate its typical habitat and to thrive in light levels prohibitive to virtually all other flowering plants.

James Napier is the author of numerous articles on biologically related subjects for journals, magazines and other publications. He has also had a number of biology textbooks published and is the author of *Teach Yourself Evolution*. He is the Chief Examiner of GCE 'A' level Biology with CCEA.

Introduction

The idea of evolution – the idea that all life is related and has descended from a common ancestor – was beginning to enter the public consciousness before 1859, the year of Darwin's ground-breaking publication whose full title was *On the Origin of Species by Means of Natural Selection, or the Preservation of Favoured Races in the Struggle for Life*. In his great work, Darwin presented a **feasible mechanism** to explain how **evolution** could take place, and he supported his theory with substantial **evidence**.

Darwin's theory of evolution explains how life has developed on earth. It postulates that all life on earth today evolved from the very simple primitive organisms that were present around 3.5 billion years ago. The main driver in evolution has been **natural selection**.

This guide looks at the process of evolution and Darwin's contribution to our understanding of it. The key question is 'Can evolution explain the development of something as complex as a human?'

1 Who was Charles Darwin?

Darwin and his theory

Charles Darwin (1809–82) is one of the most famous scientists of all time. He gathered compelling evidence for the theory that all species of life have descended from a **common ancestor**, and changed the way people think about life on earth.

He advanced the idea that new species arise over many generations from older species through a branching pattern of evolution. He called this process **natural selection**.

Darwin was the first person to support the idea of evolution with a plausible mechanism and detailed evidence

This chapter looks at the background to Darwin's work, starting with his defining five-year voyage around the world on the *HMS Beagle*. Key points covered include:

* the significance of Darwin's role as a ship's naturalist on the *HMS Beagle* in formulating his ideas
* **his development of the theory** – the 20-year delay from the *Beagle*'s return to the date of his first significant publication on evolution
* the outline of his theory of **'descent with modification'**
* the impact of the publication of his major work, *On the Origin of Species by Means of Natural Selection*.

The *HMS Beagle* expedition

Darwin dropped out of medical school and entered Cambridge, anticipating a career in the church. However, his real interest was natural history, so when offered the role of ship's naturalist on an expedition to South America aboard the *HMS Beagle* in 1831, he accepted.

In South America, Darwin observed many types of plants and animals, noting that they showed gradual variation across geographical regions. Fossils and their living relatives showed similarities, but also obvious differences.

In the **Galapagos Islands**, Darwin observed slight variations in the giant tortoises and finches between different islands. Some species were unique (**endemic**) to particular islands, even though these islands were close to other islands.

Darwin struggled to reconcile the prevailing idea of **fixity of species** – the unchanging nature of all species through time – with what he saw.

4

What could he conclude from his observations?

1 Each type of organism shows variation.
2 Fossils show that organisms have changed over time.
3 Each type of tortoise (or finch) has probably evolved from a common ancestor.

'I was much struck with certain facts in the distribution of the inhabitants of South America, and in the geological relations of the present to the past inhabitants of that continent. These facts seemed to me to throw some light on the origin of species – that mystery of mysteries.'

On the Origin of Species, Charles Darwin (1859)

Developing the theory

In the three years following his return from his voyage in 1836, Darwin developed his theory in extensive private notes not intended for publication. Using his collection of specimens and observations from the voyage and also running further experiments, he filled his notebooks with **facts** and **evidence**.

In 1842 he summarized his theory of evolution in a short account, and made a fuller version in 1844 – but again, these notes were not for publication. However, he did agree that his wife Emma would publish the 1844 version should he die.

What did he publish?

The early publications contained little about evolutionary theory.

* **1839:** *The Journal of Researches* was a travel log that focused on the *Beagle*'s voyage.
* **1840s:** he published the geological data built up during the *Beagle*'s expedition.
* **Early 1850s:** he published meticulously researched work on barnacles.

Why did he delay publishing his thoughts on evolution?

He wanted to present unarguable evidence, as he was aware of the effect this publication would have on society.

Eventually, in 1858, 20 years after he developed his theory, it was published – but even then his hand was forced.

Publication of Darwin's theory

In 1858 it became apparent that another scientist, Alfred Wallace, had independently come up with a similar theory of evolution, but without Darwin's **meticulous research** and **overwhelming evidence**. The two men agreed that they would jointly present their findings.

On 1 July they presented brief summaries of their findings to the Linnaean Society in London. The muted public reaction to their papers galvanized Darwin into action, and the following year he published his *On the Origin of Species.* Its significance became immediately apparent, and the first edition sold out on the first day.

'This preservation of favourable variations and the rejection of injurious variations, I call Natural Selection.'

On the Origin of Species, Charles Darwin (1859)

8

On the Origin of Species in a nutshell

1 All organisms of a similar type (species) vary from each other.
2 As each species produces more offspring than can survive, there is a **struggle for existence**.
3 Due to competition, the best-adapted individuals survive at the expense of the less well adapted – this is **natural selection**.
4 The best-adapted individuals are more likely to reproduce and pass their characteristics to offspring, leading to a change over time in the species.

The impact of *On the Origin of Species*

There was significant **religious opposition**. Darwin had anticipated this, so *On the Origin of Species* made little reference to man. Critics (incorrectly) suggested that Darwin was implying that '**man had descended from the apes**'.

* Darwin's theory did suggest that man and the apes are 'cousins', descended from a common ancestor.
* He addressed human evolution in a later book, *The Descent of Man* (1871).
* Eventually, Darwin had the support of many, although not all, in the **scientific community**.

Public-school educated, the son of a doctor and the grandson of Erasmus Darwin (a significant contributor to early evolutionary thinking himself), Charles had the understanding to recognize the anti-establishment nature of his views.

10

Darwin's ideas were debated in the newspapers, in scientific meetings and in church communities. By the mid-1870s most scientists accepted evolution but were more sceptical about natural selection.

CASE STUDY: Darwin's bulldog

Thomas Huxley, a vociferous supporter of Darwin (and often referred to as 'Darwin's bulldog') was involved in an oft-quoted spat with the Bishop of Oxford, Samuel Wilberforce, during a public meeting in 1860. He memorably defeated Wilberforce's attempt to pour scorn on Darwin's theory, showing that it could not easily be dismissed.

2 Natural selection

What is natural selection?

FACT!

Natural selection is a key pillar in evolutionary ~~theory~~. Darwin coined the phrase natural selection to help explain how **'descent with modification'** occurred. Natural selection explains how individuals with **beneficial adaptations** survive and pass these adaptations on to their offspring at the expense of individuals with less favourable characteristics.

'It may be said that natural selection is daily and hourly scrutinizing, throughout the world, every variation, even the slightest; rejecting that which is bad, preserving and adding up all that is good.'

On the Origin of Species, Charles Darwin (1859)

This chapter covers the following key points:

* how we can see **natural selection in action** today – and its key features
* **categories** of natural selection – stabilizing and directional
* other **types** of selection – sexual selection and artificial selection
* the idea that whole groups can be selected for, and what we mean by **'the selfish gene'**.

Natural selection is the mechanism by which evolution takes place

Natural selection in action

Darwin explained the principle of natural selection, but he couldn't show it happening.

> One everyday example is antibiotic resistance in bacteria.

How we can show natural selection in action?

* Bacteria, like other living organisms, show **variation**.
* Occasionally a very small number have a **mutation** (change to their DNA) that makes affected bacteria antibiotic resistant.
* The frequency of antibiotic-resistant bacteria is usually very low.

Why?

* Mutations are very rare events. Mutations that provide antibiotic resistance are even rarer.
* If an **antibiotic** is added, any antibiotic-resistant bacteria survive but non-resistant bacteria are killed.
* **'Superbugs'** are resistant to a number of different types of antibiotic.

Here are some key points:

1 Natural selection requires **variation** – nature needs adaptation(s) to 'favour'.
2 The variation needs to be genetic in origin (i.e. a variation in DNA) to lead to a change over time in a species.
3 Natural selection is **environmentally dependent** – an adaptation may only be favourable in a particular situation, e.g. antibiotic resistance is only an advantage to bacteria if antibiotics are used.
4 Natural selection is more intense when competition is greatest (the **struggle for existence**).

Natural selection is a non-random process that acts on random variation in individuals

Categories of natural selection
Why is evolutionary change as a result of natural selection not more evident?

Evolutionary change is slow, but this is not the whole story. In species well adapted to their environment, natural selection will favour the status quo, **stabilizing selection**.

CASE STUDY: Birth weight and natural selection

A famous investigation in a London hospital in 1978 demonstrated this type of selection.

* Babies with average birth weights survived best.
* Mortality rates were higher for *both* very small and very large babies.

Babies of average birth weight survived best because they were best adapted (at least at the birth stage).

Stabilizing selection is very common in nature.

Directional selection is where natural selection favours a character extreme.

Prey animals, such as rabbits or zebra, need to be on their guard against predators. Natural selection will favour the quickest and most agile, not the average. Over time, average speed and level of agility are likely to increase in both predators and prey – the so-called evolutionary '**arms race**'.

What other example of directional selection have we come across?

Antibiotic resistance in bacteria.

Sexual selection

Sexual selection is a sub-set of natural selection, important in species where females produce fewer eggs than males do sperm. Such females must be selective in their choice of mate, to help ensure breeding success.

This type of selection usually ensures that the best-adapted males mate with females.

5　Typically, females **select** males on the basis of their 'good genes', as seen by their having the best plumage or other attractive feature.
6　Males also **compete** with each other in sexual selection.

20

Artificial selection

Virtually all domestic plants and animals today look so different from their ancestors as to be unrecognizable. This is as a result of **artificial selection** through selective breeding by humans.

Feature	Natural selection	Artificial selection
Selection agent	Nature	Man
Rate of change in species	Usually slow	Usually rapid

People have carried out selective breeding for centuries, but we can now also change organisms through:

* **cloning** – producing organisms with the same DNA
* **genetic modification (GM)** – crops that have had specific DNA sequences inserted to produce characteristics favourable to humans.

Artificial selection of other organisms is invariably for the benefit of humans. Embryo selection is an example of artificial selection in humans.

Selection at different levels

Does natural selection favour individuals or the beneficial genetic material they contain?

In the presence of an antibiotic:

* antibiotic-resistant bacteria survive
* non-resistant bacteria are killed.

This example shows that **individuals** survive or die due to natural selection.

In *The Selfish Gene*, first published in 1976, Richard Dawkins proposed that natural selection tends to favour or reject individual genes because it is the genes that ultimately determine an organism's characteristics.

In effect, he proposed that individuals were really 'vehicles' for their genes, and that natural selection acts to preserve the best **genetic material**.

Selecting the family – kin selection

Many insects live in tight social groups, where some individuals, for example worker bees, don't reproduce and 'sacrifice' themselves for the **benefit of the group**.

How does natural selection favour self-sacrificing organisms that don't reproduce?

* The workers help close relatives (other bees) that have very similar genes.
* Their selfless actions aid their own survival by maintaining the hive.
* Their actions also aid the survival of other bees that pass on genes (almost) identical to those of the workers.

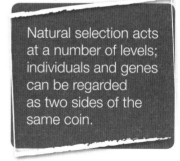

Natural selection acts at a number of levels; individuals and genes can be regarded as two sides of the same coin.

3 Species and speciation

New species

For evolution to be true, it must include the formation of new biological **species**. This is called **speciation**. A species is a specific type of living organism that has features making it distinct from all other life forms. A species differs from other groupings such as sub-species or races.

What is the process of speciation, and what are the factors needed for it to happen?

Speciation is the mechanism that produces new species

. . . .

In this chapter we will cover:

* the **species concept** – what is a species?
* the different **types of speciation**: allopatric, parapatric and sympatric
* **reproductive isolation** – the key requirement necessary for speciation.

'When I view all beings not as special creations, but as the lineal descendants of some few beings which lived long before the first bed of the Silurian system was deposited, they seem to me to become ennobled.'

On the Origin of Species, Charles Darwin (1859)

What is a species?

There are over 300 different types of dog.

Is each type

- ✗ *a species?*
- ✗ *a sub-species?*
- ✗ *a race?*
- ✔ *a breed?*

So what is a species?

A species is a group of organisms that share ancestry and in natural conditions can **interbreed** to produce **fertile offspring**. There is only one dog species, and theoretically dogs of any two different breeds can mate.

A species is a group of organisms that can interbreed to produce fertile offspring

Some terms used for species sub-groups

Breed	Usually developed through artificial selection
Race	A term for sub-groups in some species, e.g. man
Sub-species	Often different enough to suggest that they could diverge into separate species

In many organisms there is a continuum from sub-group variation through to species. It is often difficult to identify where the species boundary exists.

Do dogs really fit our definition of a single species?   Yes.

For many organisms, for example some orchids, it is very difficult, or even almost impossible, to determine whether they are a species or sub-species. Is this important?

Allopatric speciation

This is the most **common** form of speciation and usually has the following sequence:

1 Two or more populations of a species become **geographically separated**.
2 The two populations no longer interbreed.
3 There is no **gene flow** between the separate populations.
4 The populations diverge as:
  a genetic differences build up in each population
  b natural selection acts in a different way in each area (population).
5 Eventually the populations diverge to the extent that they cannot interbreed, even if they are no longer separated. Once this happens they are separate species.

The founder effect

A particular type of allopatric speciation is referred to as the **founder effect**.

If, for example, a **small** population of a species becomes (permanently) isolated from the main group, the two groups are likely to diverge, as with normal allopatric speciation.

However, it is possible that the **gene pool** (range of genes present) in the smaller population is not representative of the species as a whole – likely if only a few individuals are involved.

With the founder effect, speciation is aided by the following differences in the two populations:

* the different genetic starting points
* different rates and types of genetic change
* different natural selection pressures.

Parapatric speciation

This occurs when different populations of the same species co-exist along a common border.

1 Gene flow between the two populations takes place, but is insignificant compared to their **very different selection pressures**.
2 The populations on each side of the border become adapted through natural selection for their particular environment, and individuals from the other population are much less adapted and unable to become established.
3 Eventually the differences in the two populations can be reinforced through different flowering periods, etc.

Parapatric speciation can be seen in populations of some grass species that co-exist along the boundary of land contaminated by heavy metals, e.g. between mine spoil heaps and uncontaminated land.

Sympatric speciation

In sympatric speciation different populations are *not* geographically isolated but have different '**preferences**' within the same area.

CASE STUDY: Apple maggot flies

In North America the larvae of apple maggot flies traditionally developed inside the fruit of hawthorn. About 150 years ago some apple maggot flies were found to be completing their life cycles on apple trees. Apple trees are not native to America but were introduced by Europeans.

The two groups of fly can co-exist geographically, but there is little gene flow because they have different habitats. Genetic differences have become reinforced as their life cycles have evolved in tandem with the different flowering times of their preferred host.

The importance of reproductive isolation in speciation

All methods of speciation have one thing in common.

Each of the types of speciation involves the development of **barriers** to restrict or stop gene flow between populations.

> Speciation requires reproductive isolation between two or more populations of a species.

For new species to form, the populations need to be **reproductively isolated** from each other to establish two separate gene pools.

'Take the Galapagos. Among its 13 islands there are 28 species of birds found nowhere else.'

Why Evolution is True, Jerry Coyne (2009)

Why are there so many endemic (unique) species on oceanic islands?

Reinforcing reproductive isolation

Following initial geographical or other isolation of populations, differential natural selection invariably leads to other reproductive isolation mechanisms or barriers in time.

These can be before (**prezygotic**) or after (**postzygotic**) the egg is fertilized.

Examples include:

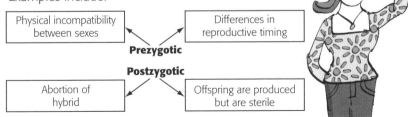

| Physical incompatibility between sexes | | Differences in reproductive timing |

Prezygotic

Postzygotic

| Abortion of hybrid | | Offspring are produced but are sterile |

4 Darwin's gaps

'Difficulties on theory'

Darwin knew that gaps existed in both his theory of the mechanism of evolution and the supporting evidence. This is hardly surprising, as Darwin produced his theory over 150 years ago.

His chapter 6 of *On the Origin of Species,* called *'Difficulties on Theory',* reflects the fact that he had relatively little background scientific knowledge, especially at the crucial **biochemical** and **microscopic** level. Since then scientific knowledge has grown exponentially.

Darwin knew that gaps existed in both his theory of evolution and the evidence

This chapter covers the following key points:

* Darwin had no understanding about **DNA, genes and chromosomes** and the mechanism of **heredity**.
* He had no knowledge of **mutations**.
* He had no **evidence** of natural selection (or evolution) taking place.
* He worried about the strength of evidence:
  » in the fossil record
  » that natural selection could form complex organisms.

'...why, if species have descended from other species by insensibly fine gradations, do we not everywhere see innumerable transitional forms? Why is not all nature in confusion ...?'

On the Origin of Species, Charles Darwin (1859)

The mechanism of heredity – Darwin's missing link

The **mechanism of heredity** (passing of characteristics from parents to offspring) was a blank sheet to Darwin.

To make things worse it was assumed that inheritance involved **blending**, producing offspring with characteristics midway between their parents.

40

Why is blending a problem when explaining natural selection or evolution?

*Because blending **decreases variation** rather than increases it – the raw material on which selection acts.*

Even more disappointing was that **Gregor Mendel**, an Austrian monk, had worked out the process of heredity around the time that Darwin was producing his theory of natural selection. However, Darwin was not aware of Mendel's research.

Mutations – the life blood of evolution

DNA had not been discovered in Darwin's time. **Mutations** are changes to an organism's DNA.

We have met mutations before – remember antibiotic resistance in bacteria. Mutations are important to natural selection because:

1 they can produce **large** changes in organisms
2 they can produce **novel** characteristics
3 they can pass from parent to offspring
4 some variation produced could be **beneficial**.

Why is only the beneficial variation important in evolution?

Harmful variation will be eliminated by natural selection. Mutations are important because they produce large and novel variation on which natural selection acts.

Observing change taking place

Darwin had to work backwards. He could see the **products** of natural selection and evolution, but had to work out his theory by deduction. Today we have abundant evidence of natural selection and evolution in action. Think of:

* antibiotic resistance in bacteria
* the rapidly evolving HIV viruses
* new flu strains
* pesticide resistance in insects.

CASE STUDY: Evolution in action 1

Richard Lenski and colleagues at Michigan State University have been culturing *E. coli* bacteria continuously since 1988. They have identified genes that have mutated to make the bacteria better adapted. The bacteria now grow much faster than the original population and use nutrients more efficiently.

We are unlikely to see evidence of human evolution over a period of a few decades. However, there is plenty of evidence of it happening in our recent past.

CASE STUDY: Evolution in action 2

Young babies possess the enzyme lactase to digest milk, their only food source. Normally we lose the ability to produce lactase after we are weaned, and can even develop 'lactose intolerance'. Why?

Milk was a very insignificant part of our diet a few thousand years ago. In many human populations the DNA mutation that maintained lactase production evolved in parallel with the domestication of cows and the availability of milk.

We have abundant evidence of evolution in action

Missing links – gaps in the fossils?

'That our paleontological collections are very imperfect, is admitted by every one.'

On the Origin of Species, Charles Darwin (1859)

If evolution is true, fossil evidence should show the intermediate life forms between modern species and their extinct ancestors. Darwin struggled to find these '**missing links**'.

Where's the fossil evidence?

> *Few organisms form fossils, and conditions need to be just right for fossilization.*

> *It's been estimated that we've found fossils for less than 1% of all the species that have existed.*

Dinosaurs are easy to spot!
What are the chances of a non-expert
identifying most other fossils?

Many fossils are destroyed
by geological activity and
construction work.

Darwin was worried by the sudden appearance of
large numbers of species appearing together in
the fossil record. Was this creation, not evolution?

* An example is the '**Cambrian Explosion**'.
  We now know that this 'sudden appearance'
  involved up to 20 million years!
* Older rocks do have fossils – but they are
  simpler life forms and harder to find. During
  the Cambrian Period many animals evolved
  hard skeletons, making fossilization easier.

Problem solved.

Difficulty with complexity

It is easy to comprehend that natural selection favours increasing agility in a predator. However, it is a very different matter to believe that natural selection is the mechanism that produces the most complex organs.

The philosophy of 'natural theology' was in vogue during Darwin's time. A key contribution to this was William Paley's book *Natural Theology* (1802), which gloried in the complexity of natural history but clearly attributed this to the work of God.

This argument in recent decades has been rebranded 'Intelligent Design' (see chapter 7).

> *How could very complex organs such as the human eye evolve incrementally? It is either an eye or it is not!*

Darwin understood that **many** incremental steps are needed to produce complex organs. The work of other scientists adds support.

* **Radioactive dating** shows that the earth is **4.5 billion years old**.
* Time is needed for natural selection to produce complex organs.
* Organs are not '**all or nothing**'.

The types of eye in the animal kingdom range from simple eye spots that can distinguish light and shade to the very complex eye of human beings.

The different types are an advantage to all the organisms that possess them. The ability to distinguish between light and dark in some very simple organisms is an advantage favoured by selection.

5 Variation and natural selection

Why are we all so different?

Variation is the raw material of natural selection; but it is the **genetic** and not the **environmental** variation that is important. Genetics is the study of the structure and role of DNA and the significance of gamete (sex cell) production and fertilization to variation. With a basic understanding of genetics you'll see that sex is the crucible of genetic novelty.

Sex is the crucible of genetic novelty
· ·

This chapter covers the following key points:

* the difference between **genetic** and **environmental** variation
* the structure and function of **DNA**
* the principle of **genetics** – how our DNA is passed through the generations
* the role of **sex** – mixing the gene pot
* changes to our DNA – the causes and effects of **mutations**
* the **importance** of variation.

What is DNA?

DNA is the molecule of heredity
(the genetic code). Key facts
about DNA are:

* Its structure is a **double helix**.
* It is described as the
  universal code, present in all
  living organisms.
* Its key components are
  called **bases** (denoted A, T, C
  and G).

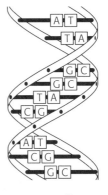

Note that
bases A–T
and C–G
only combine
together

● The double helix of DNA

Each individual organism has **unique** DNA. The more closely individuals
(or species) are related the more similarities they have in their DNA
sequence.

* The bases along one side (strand) of DNA are read in sequences of three called **base triplets**. In our example ATC, CAG, etc. are base triplets.
* Each group of three bases in sequence codes for an amino acid.
* Amino acids are built up into proteins.

* Proteins are the building blocks of organisms.
* A section of DNA that codes for a particular protein or characteristic is a **gene**.
* Genes are built up into **chromosomes**.
* Humans have 46 chromosomes in each cell. This is a lot of DNA.

It is the sequence of bases along one strand of DNA that provides the genetic code.

The genetics of variation

✳ **Mendel** was able to explain how (some) characteristics in organisms passed through the generations.

✳ He investigated how some characteristics such as flower colour passed from parent to offspring.

✳ He concluded that characteristics were controlled by factors (genes) that pass from parents to offspring.

> Genetic characteristics in organisms are a consequence of the DNA mix that results when DNA from each parent combines during fertilization.

Environmental variation, for example changes in plant growth caused by different levels of light intensity, is subject to natural selection, but plays no part in evolution, since these characteristics do not pass to offspring.

Why can siblings in a family differ so much?

*The answer is **sex**.*

Each of us can produce millions of different types of sex cell in a process called **meiosis**.

✳ Most human body cells contain 46 chromosomes in 23 pairs.
✳ Sex cells (sperm or eggs) have 23 chromosomes. One and only one must be from each pair.
✳ Either chromosome of one pair can combine with either in another pair, and so on. Therefore each person can have 2^{23} **possible chromosome combinations** in their sex cells.

Consider that our partner's sex cells show the same variation.

Think of the number of possible chromosome (DNA) combinations when two sex cells combine during **fertilization**. Fertilization restores the 46 chromosomes arranged in 23 pairs.

Mutations

Sex is excellent at 'mixing up' DNA and providing new combinations.

Mutations are changes beyond what sex can provide. There are two types of mutation:

* **chromosome mutations** – these are big changes and can affect entire chromosomes. For example, Down syndrome is a consequence of each cell having 47 chromosomes instead of 46
* **gene mutations** – these usually involve a small number of bases.

'Genetic variation generated by mutation is widespread: mutant forms of genes, for example, explain ... variation in height, weight, biochemistry, and innumerable other traits.'

Why Evolution is True, Jerry Coyne (2009)

Key facts about mutations

1 Most mutations are **harmful**.
2 Most occur when cells are dividing, e.g. making sex cells.
3 Mutations can occur **spontaneously**.
4 Mutation rates can be accelerated by certain environmental factors, including UV light and X-rays.

It is the very infrequent beneficial mutation that is important in evolution

While mutations in an organism tend to be disruptive, if the environment changes mutations can prove advantageous, and it is the very infrequent beneficial mutation that is important in evolution.

Sickle cell anaemia – a beneficial mutation?

Sickle cell anaemia is a serious blood condition caused by a gene mutation. Affected people have **abnormal haemoglobin**, which is less efficient at carrying oxygen.

Category	Effect
Normal (no mutation)	Normal oxygen transport by blood
One copy of mutant gene	Blood less efficient at carrying oxygen but individuals survive
Two copies of mutant gene	Blood inefficient at carrying oxygen – reduced life expectancy

Why is the number of people with the mutant gene negligible in normal circumstances?

Individuals with the mutant gene are selected against, and relatively few have children allowing the mutant gene to perpetuate.

However, in some parts of the world where malaria is common it has been found that many more people have one copy of the mutant gene.

Explanation: individuals with one copy of the gene (carriers) may get out of breath easily due to their poor oxygen carrying capacity, but they:

✳ have a degree of **resistance** or tolerance to malaria
✳ show **less severe symptoms** when infected.

Therefore individuals with one mutant gene are selected for by natural selection.

This example reminds us of another key point about natural selection: it is dependent on environmental conditions. A sickle cell anaemia gene is only an advantage in areas where malaria is common.

6 Evidence for evolution

The accumulating evidence

Evolution is still sometimes hotly debated, particularly in the USA and in fundamentalist evangelical circles. However, compelling evidence for evolution is increasing almost daily, and comes in many forms: **fossil, biogeographical, anatomical, molecular and genetic.**

Darwin's insight is all the more remarkable as most of the evidence has only come to light since he published his theory. There is one consistent theme: the accumulating evidence increasingly supports, and never contradicts, the theory of evolution.

The accumulating evidence supports and never contradicts the theory of evolution

This chapter covers the following key points:

* the **fossil evidence** – there is no shortage of 'missing links' now
* **the geographical distribution** of species – the evidence of the continents and the islands
* the **anatomical evidence** – the evidence within our bodies
* the **molecular evidence** – the evidence at a microscopic level
* the question of whether evolution is still only a **theory**.

64

CASE STUDY: Missing links found

Archaeopteryx fossils are about 150 million years old. Archaeopteryx is 'part reptile, part bird', having lived in the period when birds evolved from dinosaurs (reptiles).

Tiktaalik roseae fossils, discovered In 2004, are 375 million years old. They show many fish-like features – scales and fins – but have skeletons more typical of four-legged vertebrates living on land. *Tiktaalik* shows a key stage in the evolution of land-dwelling vertebrates from fish.

Many 'missing links' are missing no more!

What about human fossils?

In Darwin's time there was virtually no fossil evidence to show an evolutionary link between humans and the apes. Since then we have discovered fossils for about 20 ancestral species that arose after our split from the apes.

These fossils have clear **gradations of complexity**, and show:

1 the evolution of **bipedalism** (walking on two legs)
2 **increasing skull and brain size**
3 **changes in dentition** to match dietary changes.

Anatomically modern humans appeared long before 'cultural' traits such as the creation of art and music, religious practices and tool-making techniques, evidence for which did not appear in the archaeological record until around 50,000 years ago.

The biogeographical evidence

Animal and plant species on different continents differ considerably, even within the same climate and latitude. For example, Africa has 'Old World' short-tailed monkeys, whereas South America has 'New World' longer-tailed monkeys.

66

CASE STUDY: Marsupial mammals in Australia

Marsupial mammals are almost entirely restricted to Australia, with placental mammals elsewhere. The 200 marsupial species have features in common that are not seen in placental mammals.

The only possible explanation for this is that the wide range of marsupials has evolved from a common ancestor, filling **niches** (roles) in Australia normally taken by placental species elsewhere.

Life on islands helps us understand the concepts of isolation, natural selection and speciation. It also provides superb evidence for evolution.

* **Hawaii** has many species of endemic insects, including nearly half the world's species of the fruit fly *Drosophila*, but no native reptiles or mammals.
* **Madagascar** has 37 species of lemur, and most of its reptiles and amphibians are endemic, but it has no elephants, zebras or giraffes as found in nearby Africa.

How can island life be explained?

Reproductive isolation allowed species to evolve from the few species that originally colonized the islands.

Island life shows the concept of **adaptive radiation,** with species evolving to fill all the ecological niches.

The evidence within us

Humans start life as a **fish-like embryo** because we evolved from a fish-like ancestor. The covering of downy hair that we develop while in the womb and shed before birth is evidence of our primate ancestry.

Vestigial organs such as the appendix provide further clues. The appendix may or may not have a minor role now, but it does not have the role for which it originally evolved – as a fermenting chamber in our herbivorous past.

Snakes with vestigial legs, burrowing and cave-dwelling animals with vestigal eyes that don't function?

The only explanation is that natural selection gradually eliminates redundant structures.

How can we explain the following?

* **The inverted retinas in vertebrates**
  Light rays pass through nerve cells (wiring) *before* reaching the light-sensitive cells of the retina – the other way round would be better.

* **The complexity of human birth**
  As we evolved larger heads, birth through the pelvis has become (before modern medicine) risky and painful.

* **The gap between the ovaries and the oviducts**
  Would it not be better to have these joined? There is no biological reason why they couldn't be.

> Natural selection doesn't go back to the drawing board; it can only modify what is there.

The molecular evidence

DNA is the **universal code** suggesting a common ancestor. Biochemical processes – such as enzyme action and respiration – are basically similar in all organisms. This is further evidence of a common ancestor.

Mutations in DNA occur at a fairly consistent rate, so they can be thought of as **'molecular clocks'**. Similarity in DNA between different types of organism correlates closely with other evidence concerning the closeness of their relationship.

The evidence for evolution is irrefutable!

*Why is it still called the **theory** of evolution?*

Evolution is a theory in the same way as we think of the theory of relativity, theory of music exams or even mathematical theories.

The 'theory' refers to the explanatory role. The **theory** of evolution explains the **process** of evolution.

✔ *Is evolution a fact?*
✔ *Is evolution a theory?*

Evolution is both a fact and a theory!

However, not everyone believes the theory of evolution to be true. The next chapter will try to explain why.

7 The arguments against evolution

Opposition to evolution

Despite the strength of evidence to support evolution, it has nowhere near universal acceptance. Several arguments are currently used to oppose the theory of evolution. These include the debate surrounding the origin of life itself. It also helps to explain why many famous contemporary scientists believe in both evolution and **God**.

The idea of evolution is still opposed by many people

This chapter covers the following key points:

* the social and religious background at the time of the publication of *On the Origin of Species*
* biological **complexity**, a key pillar in the arguments of supporters of intelligent design
* the **origin of life** itself, before evolution had anything to work on
* the reasons why many scientists, from Darwin's time to the present, accept evolution but suggest that it is not the whole explanation to account for life on earth.

The historical context

In the early 19th century most people believed that:

* the earth was created 6,000 years ago
* the natural world showcased God's work
* man had a unique place in nature.

It gradually became apparent that:

* **the earth was much older** (significant in 'setting the scene' for Darwin's theory as it provided the **time** needed for evolution to occur)
* fossils showed evidence of **change with time**.

Some argued that this could be explained through a sequence of 'successive creations'. It was not a great leap forward to suggest that organisms changed in a predetermined pattern following a set of natural laws developed by God.

Opposition to the ideas of *On the Origin of Species* was largely due to:

✳ hostility to the role of natural selection because it meant that:
  » there was no requirement for God
  » it was not 'purposeful' – there was no 'goal'
✳ the requirement to believe that man was just another 'animal'.

Many scientists and theologians could not accept that man's higher mental powers and moral code or sense of right and wrong could be explained by natural selection. Some believed in **theistic evolution** – evolution directed by God.

Since then, nearly all criticisms of evolution have come from religious sources rather than from the scientific community. Some religious people still believe that a deity supernaturally created the world largely in its current form.

Complexity: the argument of intelligent design

The intelligent design (ID) movement is largely based in the USA. Advocates of the ID movement argue that evolution alone cannot explain the **complexity of life**.

They tend to avoid defending the impossible, accepting the age of the earth and that evolution through common descent has occurred. Battles focus on the ability of natural selection to explain the complexity of biological structures, especially those at a molecular level. Key areas for attack have included the eye and complex microscopic and molecular body parts.

ID supporters argue that the earth has amazingly 'finely tuned' life-supporting conditions (known as the '**Goldilock's zone**'), while the rest of the universe seems largely barren.

While not directly linked to evolution, the statistically staggering improbability that this happened by chance is used to support the argument of design.

The case for intelligent design is, however, failing. It is under attack from:

* many Christians and others, who see it as being too **mechanistic**
* the fact that supporters of ID don't necessarily specify **who the 'designer' is**
* accumulating **evidence** that evolution *can* account for the complexity of life on earth.

> ### '...geology plainly declares that all species have changed; and they have changed in the manner which my theory requires.'
>
> *On the Origin of Species*, Charles Darwin (1859)

The origin of life

Natural selection acts on pre-existing life forms. No one knows for sure how life originated, but we can make some **educated predictions**. We can be fairly sure that:

1 the environmental conditions needed to be right
2 the raw materials needed to be there
3 the probability was so small that it took many millions of years to happen
4 it only needed to happen once.

> Life originated from simple inorganic forms over 3,500 million years ago.

Natural selection cannot explain the origin of life itself

CASE STUDY: Replicating the start of life

In 1953 Stanley Miller (University of Chicago) devised an experiment to show how life could have originated (the Miller Urey experiment).

He used ammonia, methane, hydrogen and water in a mixture resembling the **'primeval soup'** conditions on earth when life originated. A continual electrical charge simulated lightning (energy source). After a week some of the amino acids essential for life had been synthesized from the mixture.

Other scientists continued the work, and after a few years all the amino acids had been produced from inorganic molecules. Although making amino acids is a long way from making a living organism, Miller's experiment shows how some of the steps may have occurred.

Where are we now?

* Many of the positions held at the time of Darwin have not changed much.
* Many creationists accept the literal word of the Bible and don't accept the geological or biological evidence for evolution.
* A growing number of modern theologians accept the overwhelming **evidence for evolution** and argue that it can be reconciled with religious belief.
* Although their exact positions vary, many suggest that the following provide **evidence of God**:
  » the 'unique' nature of man – our ability to use language and make sense of the world
  » religious concepts including the 'soul', 'original sin' and 'salvation'
  » man's sense of right and wrong (our moral code).

For many people, the focus for evolution is no longer whether it occurred, or even the strength of the evidence. There is still debate over aspects of the mechanism.

Science is still throwing light on many of the other great mysteries, including the origin of the universe.

> **'There are many scientists who still have deeply held religious beliefs, and many religious thinkers who are happy to accept evolution. Evolutionism is not necessarily atheistic, and creationism is not the only alternative open to the Christian.'**
>
> *Monkey Trials and Gorilla Sermons,* Peter Bowler (2007)

Evolution is a fact – debates over other issues have no bearing on that fact.

8 The tree of life

Diversity and complexity

The idea of a 'tree of life' illustrates the concept that all life on earth is related. Darwin's *On the Origin of Species* contained just one illustration, a branched diagram like a tree.

Over time, an increasing number of types of organisms appeared on earth, providing ever-increasing **diversity**. If evolution is true, we would also expect growing **complexity** over time, as organisms change and become better adapted to their environment.

Descent with modification best explains the 'tree of life'

● ●

This chapter explains the pattern of the tree of life, outlines some of its key stages and reviews the methods used to analyse evolutionary relationships between organisms. Key points covered are:

* explanations for the tree of life
* why the tree of life is further evidence for evolution
* **extinction** (the loss of species) and man's role in speeding up the rate of extinction of species
* some of the key stages in evolution
* the DNA **molecular clock** – confirming the tree of life.

> **'Natural selection will not necessarily produce absolute perfection.'**
>
> *On the Origin of Species,* Charles Darwin (1859)

The growing tree of life

The diagram shows what happens when species split into two (**speciation**) throughout a period of time. It shows that:

1 the **number** of species tends to increase with time
2 the degree of **divergence** increases – there is a greater range of organisms today than early in evolutionary history
3 in general, ancestral species are less **complex** than their descendants.

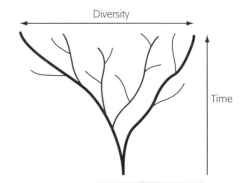

Diversity

Time

Evolution is ongoing, as there is no organism that cannot be further improved through natural selection.

88

Simplification and living fossils

There are exceptions; some types of organism become **simplified** over time:

* Snakes are reptiles that have lost their limbs through evolution.
* Some human gut parasites are simpler than their free-living forms. For example, tapeworms do not have the complex sensory systems that their free-living relatives have.

Why would a gut parasite need eyes?

'**Living fossils**' are organisms that have changed little through geological history. An excellent example is the coelacanth. Coelacanths are fish that were very common about 400 million years ago. They still exist today in small numbers, little changed from their ancestral form.

Extinction

As new species form, older species die out or become extinct. As new species evolve, they are almost by definition better adapted than their ancestral forms. These earlier forms then lose out in the **struggle for existence**.

Extinction is a natural consequence of evolutionary change

Man is becoming a major agent of extinction. Think of:

✳ man's role in the extinction of the dodo and other giant flightless birds
✳ extinction caused by habitat removal
✳ the effect of global warming.

Mass extinctions are where many species become extinct at around the same time. A common cause is **climate change**, but there are other reasons:

CASE STUDY: Extinction of the dinosaurs

The final extinction of the dinosaurs was almost certainly caused by the impact of a massive asteroid off the Yucatán peninsula in Mexico at the end of the Cretaceous Period (65 million years ago). The dust from the impact left the earth in darkness, stopping photosynthesis by plants.

The dinosaurs and many other groups became extinct at this time. However, this did provide an opportunity for others, e.g. the mammals, to evolve and fill many of the available ecological niches.

No photosynthesis = no food for animals.

Key stages in the tree of life

There have been many key stages in the development of the 'tree of life', summarized in the following table.

1 The first cells	2 More complex cells	3 Multicellular life forms
About 3.5 billion years ago	About 2 billion years ago	About 1 billion years ago
Similar to present-day bacteria	Internal structures, including a nucleus	Allow larger and more complex forms to develop
	Perhaps formed by simple cells combining	

'...the great Tree of Life...covers the surface [of the earth] with its ever-branching and beautiful ramifications.'

On the Origin of Species, Charles Darwin (1859)

The 'Cambrian Explosion'

Key stages, once bridged, can lead to rapid advancement. This could explain the **Cambrian Explosion**. Creationists have used fossil evidence of many 'new' species in the Cambrian Period (ending about 500 million years ago) as evidence of a 'creation event': most of the major invertebrate groups and the precursors of modern vertebrates appear with little or no evidence of earlier forms.

Charles Darwin considered this apparently sudden appearance of many animal groups with few or no antecedents to be the greatest single objection to his theory of evolution, but this 'explosion' of life can be explained by complex skeletal structures such as shells starting to evolve. These structures were more likely to form fossils than earlier soft-bodied forms.

Natural selection is generally believed to favour larger size, and larger creatures needed hard skeletons to provide structural support. Fossils of Pre-Cambrian forms are now being discovered as fossil recovery techniques improve.

Putting order into the tree of life

Darwin used physical similarities and differences between species to position them on the tree of life.

* Organisms can be classified in categories, or **taxa**, of increasing group size.
* **Carl Linnaeus** (1707–78) devised this classification system, and developed the **binomial names** for species, e.g. *Homo* (genus name) *sapiens* (species name).
* Different species can have the same **genus** name but only one species can have the **species** name.

> **The classification of organisms**
> species – genus – family – order – class – phylum – kingdom

The use of modern techniques

Increasingly, more sophisticated **biochemical and molecular techniques** are used to position species on the tree of life. The development of **DNA sequencing** now allows taxonomic relationships to be further analysed. Not surprisingly:

* the more closely related two species are, the more similar their DNA sequences
* DNA usually confirms relationships between species previously established on physical grounds.

9 Human evolution

Are humans unique?

Humans often don't think of themselves as animals, although we share many of our features with other species, particularly primates. What is it that sets us apart? Is it our level of **intelligence**, our sophisticated **language**, or our ability to show **empathy** that makes the difference?

Although we are different from other species, for evolution to make sense as a concept, humans have to be part of the evolutionary process.

For evolution to make sense, humans have to be part of the process

....

This chapter looks at the following key questions:

* Who are man's **closest relatives**?
* What do we know about our earliest **ancestors**?
* **Missing links and fossil evidence** – what were the major steps along the way?
* Who was **Neanderthal man**?
* What makes us so **different** from other species, and are we really unique?

Man and his primate roots

Anatomical, biochemical, molecular and DNA evidence shows that modern humans (*Homo sapiens*) are most closely related to the two chimpanzee species. As these species are found in Africa, Darwin concluded, in his 1871 work *The Descent of Man*, that it was 'probable that our early progenitors lived on the African continent'.

What do we know about our common ancestor that gave rise to both the chimpanzee and the human lines?

> It lived 5–8 million years ago.

> It lived in dense African forests.

> It was more like a chimp than a modern human.

> It was more adapted for life in trees than on open ground.

Darwin put forward the idea that humans were a twig on the tree of primate evolution, sharing a common ancestor with other primates, and most closely related to chimpanzees.

This diagram shows the **pattern of evolution** in the primates most closely related to humans. Species on the human (as opposed to the chimpanzee) branch are called **hominins**.

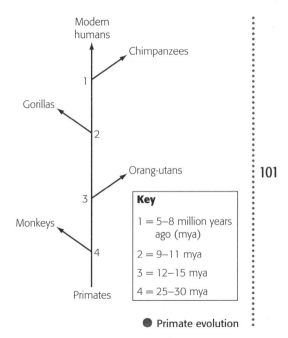

● Primate evolution

Early hominins

Some fossils of possible human ancestors, close to the chimpanzee–hominin split, include:

* *Sahelanthropus tchadensis*
    » 6–7 million years ago
    » from Chad in Africa
    » has some human (flat face), some apelike (small brain) features
    » skull set further forward on the spinal cord than in other apes, giving better balance when upright.

* *Orrorin tugenensis*
    » around 6 million years ago
    » from Kenya in Africa
    » structure of leg bone suggests it may have been bipedal (able to walk on two legs).

102

While *Sahelanthropus* and *Orrorin* might be hominins, more recent fossils have been identified that are clearly hominin. Just two examples are:

Species	Features
Australiopithecus afarensis	Well-preserved fossil (*Lucy*) discovered in 1974 provided clear evidence of bipedality. *Lucy* lived just over **3 million years ago**.
Australiopithecus africanus	Hundreds of fossils exist from southern Africa. Lived around **2.5–3 million years ago**. Slightly larger brain, and teeth more similar to modern humans than *A. afarensis*.

Chronologically, hominin fossils show distinct trends:

✔ *the development of bipedalism*
✔ *increasing brain size*

No hominin fossil find contradicts the principle that man evolved from an ape-like ancestor.

The evolution of the *Homo* genus

In the evolution of the *Homo* genus, there are three key species: *H. habilis*, *H. erectus* and *H. sapiens*.

Species	Features
Homo habilis (handy man)	Fossils dated to 2.5 million years ago Probably first hominin to use tools
Homo erectus (upright man)	Evolved around 1.8 million years ago Became extinct about 200,000 years ago Probably first hominin to use fire, allowing migration from Africa to colder climatic regions
Homo sapiens (wise man)	Evolved around 200,000 years ago Dominates the planet today

Many other hominin species **co-exist** with the extinct species above, and debate over terminology and species names continues. It is impossible to say exactly which species were our direct ancestors.

The hominin pathway shows examples of evolutionary '**dead ends**' – species that became extinct with no descendents. One such species is **Neanderthal man** (*Homo neanderthalensis*).

CASE STUDY: Neanderthal man

Neanderthal man existed from about 250,000 to 30,000 years ago, mainly in more northern areas than the evolving *H. sapiens*. Neanderthals had a shorter, stronger and more compact physique than modern humans, and were adapted to the harsh climates in which they lived.

Neanderthals co-existed with modern man, but it is still unclear whether there was any interbreeding between the two groups. It appears that *H. sapiens* out-competed the Neanderthals and so contributed to their extinction.

How are humans different from other species?

Modern humans differ from other species: we are **more intelligent**, we can appreciate **aesthetic value**, we can use **technology**, and we also use sophisticated **language**.

Are we unique, or is the difference between humans and the higher apes just a matter of degree?

Some of Darwin's supporters, including Alfred Wallace, argued that it was man's **mental capacity** that set him apart from other animals. It was what convinced them that man was a separate creation.

Darwin addressed this issue and, through well-considered argument, concluded:

'The mental faculties of man and the lower animals do not differ in kind, though immensely in degree.'

The Descent of Man, Charles Darwin (1871)

What key steps in the evolution of humans make us so different from other species?

Key steps include:

1. the evolution of **bipedalism** – its many advantages include freeing the hands to use tools
2. the development of delicate **motor skills** through the level of manual dexterity provided by an **'opposable' thumb** – the arrangement that permits grasping between thumb and the four fingers
3. increasing **brain size** – allows more effective communication, the benefits of technological advance, including in *H. erectus* the control of fire for cooking.

'Man still bears in his bodily frame the indelible stamp of his lowly origin.'

The Descent of Man, Charles Darwin (1871)

10 Evolution today – Darwin's legacy

The test of time

More than 150 years after the first publication of *On the Origin of Species*, does Darwin's theory stand the test of time?

Gaps have been filled since then, and knowledge has been updated, and though there are still many areas for debate, *On the Origin of Species* remains the **seminal work** that best explains our origins.

> ### *On the Origin of Species* remains the seminal work that best explains our origins
> ●

This chapter will review **Darwin's legacy** and his theory of evolution by natural selection. Key questions covered in this section include the following:

* Is natural selection the only mechanism that drives evolution?
* What is **genetic drift**, and how important is it?
* Does natural selection affect human societies to the extent that it affects all other species?
* How do other scientists sum up the work of Darwin, and how important is an understanding of evolution in modern-day biology?
* What is our understanding of evolution today?

Is natural selection the only explanation?

Natural selection is non-random pressures acting on random variation.

Could evolution happen by any other method?

If a population of a species is decimated by disease or predation, for example, leaving a small number left, these may not be genetically representative of the original population as a whole. As numbers increase again the new population may therefore be very different genetically from the earlier population.

This random evolutionary change is called **genetic drift** (similar in principle to the founder effect discussed earlier).

> The relative importance of natural selection and genetic drift in evolution is debatable, and probably varies from species to species.

CASE STUDY: Genetic drift in elephant seals

Northern elephant seals were hunted to near extinction by 1890, when fewer than 20 survived. Now over 30,000 exist, but they show little genetic variation, as they all are products of the surviving 20. The genetic variability (excepting mutations) is limited to the original **gene pool**.

CASE STUDY: Genetic drift in the Amish

Religious isolate groups can exemplify genetic drift. The Old Order Amish of North America are descendants of a small number of migrants from Europe. Their blood chemistry is very different from other North American populations and is evolving in isolation due to the **lack of gene flow** between different populations.

Other points to consider

Does evolution happen through gradual incremental change or short bursts of rapid change?

The answer is both. Rapid bursts of change (**punctuated equilibrium**) favour change where the environment is changing, or when a species has the opportunity to exploit new habitats.

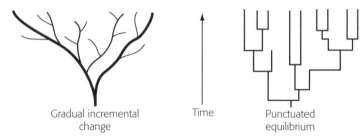

Gradual incremental change

Time

Punctuated equilibrium

Punctuated equilibrium could account for evolutionary change:

* occurring relatively rapidly
* over a short timespan
* in a few localities only.

This makes it even more difficult to locate 'transitional fossils'.

How can the effects of natural selection be reduced?

Artificial selection of animals and plants by man overrides the effect of natural selection. Think of the evolutionary effects of **socialization**. We:

* care for the weak and sick
* are living less 'fit' lifestyles as a society
* allow genes that formerly were selected against to be propagated.

'Civilization thus checks in many ways the action of natural selection.'

The Descent of Man, Charles Darwin (1871)

Darwin's other work

Darwin is most famously known for his publications relating to the voyage on the *Beagle* and the theory of evolution:

1 *The Journal of Researches* (1839) – now called the *Voyage of the Beagle*
2 *On the Origin of Species* (1859)
3 *The Descent of Man* (1871).

However, he was both versatile and prolific, writing 19 published books.

116

These publications included work on:

* barnacles
* orchids and insects
* cross- and self-fertilization in plants
* movement in plants
* insectivorous plants
* variation under domestication
* formation of vegetable mould by earthworms
* expression of the emotions.

In essence, Darwin produced ground-breaking research in many biological and biologically related fields, including psychology with *The Expression of the Emotions in Man and Animals* (1872). This work links the expression of emotions in both humans and animals to evolutionary biology. Later scientific research has in most respects supported Darwin's arguments.

The legacy of Charles Darwin

Charles Darwin's is perhaps Britain's greatest scientist. He:

* explained how evolution could happen
* allowed us to challenge our origins and our role in the world.

'*The Origin of Species* is, without doubt, the most famous book in science.'
Darwin's Island, Steve Jones (2009)

As for evolution itself, the evidence is beyond doubt, irrefutable. It can only be opposed on fundamentalist, not rational grounds.

As for evolution itself, the evidence is beyond doubt

Its status may be succinctly summarized as follows:

Around 3.5 billion years ago life evolved to give a single primitive species that became ancestral to the tree of life, with natural selection being the primary driver of change.

At the heart of evolutionary theory is the idea that life has existed for billions of years and changed over time. Related organisms share similarities derived from common ancestors. Every piece of new scientific research that impacts on evolution provides further support for the theory.

The debate now is not whether evolution is true, but whether we have evolved into a species capable of protecting our planet and caring for our many relatives on the **increasingly fragile tree of life**. Have our morals evolved in tandem with our ability to dominate all other species?

'There is grandeur in this view of life…that, whilst this planet has gone cycling on…from so simple a beginning endless forms most beautiful and most wonderful have been, and are being, evolved.'

On the Origin of Species, Charles Darwin (1859)

Further reading

The books by Darwin are still in print with a range of publishers. Some versions are abridged and often contain explanatory forewords or editor's notes.

Behe, M. J., *The Edge of Evolution – The Search for the Limits of Darwinism* (New York: Free Press, 2007)

Bowler, P J., *Monkey Trials and Gorilla Sermons - Evolution and Christianity from Darwin to Intelligent Design* (Harvard: Harvard University Press, 2007)

Coyne, J., *Why Evolution is True* (Oxford: Oxford University Press, 2009)

Davies, P., The *Goldilocks Enigma – Why is the Universe Just Right for Life?* (London: Allen Lane, 2006)

Dawkins, R., *Climbing Mount Improbable* (London: Penguin, 1996)

Dawkins, R., *Unweaving the Rainbow* (London: Penguin, 1998)

Dawkins, R., *The Ancestor's Tale – A Pilgrimage to the Dawn of Life* (London: Weidenfeld and Nicholson, 2004)

Dawkins, R., *The God Delusion* (London: Bantam Press, 2006)

Dennett, D. C., *Darwin's Dangerous Idea – Evolution and the Meanings of Life* (London: Allen Lane, 1995)

Diamond, J., *The Third Chimpanzee – The Evolution and Future of the Human Animal* (London: Harper, 1992)

Futuyma, D. J., *Evolution* (Sunderland, Mass: Sinauer Associates, 2005)

Jones, S., *Almost Like a Whale – The Origin of Species, updated* (London: Doubleday, 1999)

Lockwood, C., *The Human Story* (London: Natural History Museum, 2007)

Shubin, N., *Your Inner Fish – A Journey into the 3.5 Billion-year History of the Human Body* (London: Allen Lane, 2008)